LET'S VISIT FORMOSA

LET'S VISIT FORMOSA

Island Home of Free China

JOHN C. CALDWELL

The John Day Company
New York

© 1956 by John C. Caldwell

All rights reserved. This book, or parts thereof, must not be reproduced in any form without permission. Published by The John Day Company, 62 West 45th Street, New York 36, N. Y., and on the same day in Canada by Longmans, Green & Company, Toronto.

Pictures courtesy of the information office, International Cooperation Administration, Mission to China.

Library of Congress Catalog Card Number: 56-5976

Contents

LET'S VISIT FORMOSA

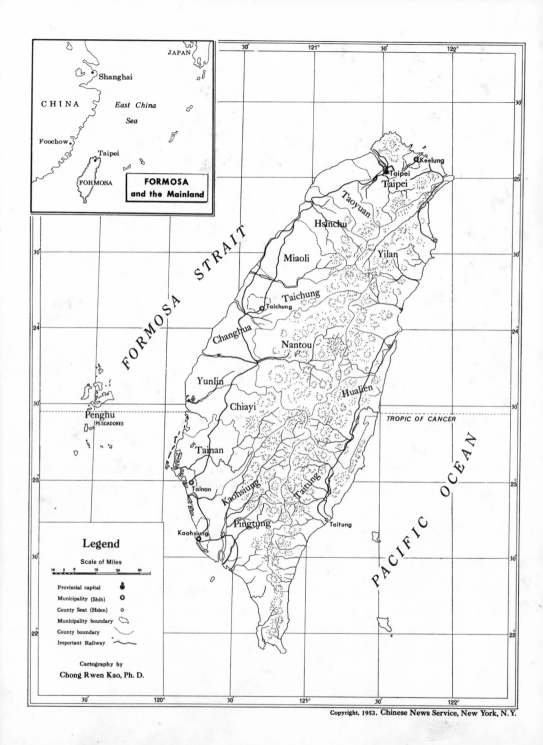

JAPAN

Shanghai

CHINA   East China
          Sea

Foochow

Taipei

FORMOSA

FORMOSA
and the Mainland

FORMOSA STRAIT

Keelung
Taipei
Taipei

Taoyuan

Hsinchu

Miaoli

Yilan

Taichung
Taichung

Changhua

Nantou

Yunlin

Hualien

Chiayi

Penghu
PESCADORES

Tainan
Tainan

Kaohsiung

Taitung

Kaohsiung
Pingtung   Taitung

TROPIC OF CANCER

PACIFIC OCEAN

Legend

Scale of Miles

Provincial capital
Municipality (Shih)
County Seat (Hsien)
Municipality boundary
County boundary
Important Railway

Cartography by
Chong Rwen Kao, Ph. D.

The Beautiful Island

IF YOU look at the map on the opposite page you see that Formosa is an island. It is about 240 miles long, shaped something like a banana. To the north lies Japan, to the south the Philippine Islands. And very close by, to the west, is the mainland of China. Formosa is not a very large island. There are about ten million people living there, fewer than in the state of New York. Why then is it important? And what's it like?

The people who live on Formosa are mostly Chinese. And Formosa is a part of China. It is the home of *Nationalist China;* or, as some people call it, *Free China.* China and the Chinese people have always been friendly to America. But now mainland China is a Communist-ruled nation. Its soldiers fought our soldiers in Korea. The people of China are still our friends. But the Communist government is not friendly. That is one reason why Formosa is important.

Another reason for Formosa's importance is its position between Japan and the Philippine Islands. Both of these countries are our allies. If Formosa were captured by a nation unfriendly to us, it would not be good, for the enemy could then threaten both Japan and the Republic of the Philippines.

It is important, then, that we know more about Formosa, its people and its history. Let's begin with the name. There are two names for the island. In the year 1517 a fleet of Portuguese ships sailed by Formosa. When the Portuguese sailors saw Formosa's lovely mountains they named the island "Ihla Formosa." This

Formosa, the beautiful island.

means "the beautiful island." Most Americans know it by this name. But the Chinese who live there call it *Taiwan,* which means "terraced bay."

Both names help describe the island. It has not one "terraced bay" but many. And it is indeed beautiful. There are actually about eighty islands in the Formosa group. Off the eastern coast there are several small and unimportant islands. And about twenty-five miles off the west coast there is a group of small islands. These, too, have two names. English-speaking people call these the *Pescadores Islands*. The Chinese call the islands *Penghu*.

There is an interesting Chinese legend about how Formosa was made. The Chinese say that many hundreds of years ago there were five dragons living under a river in China. One day the dragons decided to go exploring. They traveled under the river and out into the ocean. Then they came to the place where Formosa is now. There the dragons began to play. They chased each other. They played so hard that their tails stirred up the

Most of Formosa is mountainous.

rocks on the bottom of the ocean. The big rocks came to the surface—and created the mountains of Formosa.

Of course we don't believe this story. But Formosa does have many rocks and high mountains. And many Chinese believe that the five dragons still live in the mountains. Formosa has many earthquakes, about one each day of the year. The Chinese say the earthquakes are caused by the dragons' moving their tails.

Look once again at the map. Notice the shaded area. This is the mountainous part of the island. About two-thirds of Formosa is mountainous. In fact, except for a narrow strip along the western coast, facing China, all of Formosa is covered by mountains and hills. The mountains are very high. There are seventy-seven peaks over 10,000 feet high. The highest mountain is over 13,000 feet high. Mount Whitney, highest peak in the United States, is 14,495 feet in elevation.

Everywhere there is jungle, too. The higher mountains are covered by vast forests. In the jungles and forests are many wild animals—deer, monkeys, bear. There are lovely flowers including many kinds of wild orchids. Formosa lies within the tropics. The climate is quite warm, there is much rain. This is good for growing bananas, pineapples and oranges. In the mountains there are tea plantations. In the plains and in the valleys are rich rice fields, called *paddies*. In the south there are thousands of acres of sugar cane. If you like sweets and fresh fruit, you'll like Formosa.

The soil is so rich, the climate so good, that in many places it is possible to grow three crops each year. This is another reason why Formosa is important. The farmers grow so much rice there

There are rich plains along the West Coast.

is plenty to sell to other countries. The same is true of tea, sugar and fruit. Formosa is one of the most fertile places in the world.

Formosa Long Ago

Another way to learn about a country is to study its history. We now know what Formosa looks like. Its history is interesting and exciting. And you will be surprised that its history is quite like our own. Many foreign nations wanted Formosa. Colonists were sent from Europe. The Spanish and the Dutch once ruled

13

parts of the island. English, German and American soldiers and sailors invaded it. A French fleet of warships once attacked the island. Then, after a war between China and Japan, Formosa was ruled by the Japanese for many years. After the end of World War II Japan was defeated and Formosa again became a *province* (state) of China.

Think of it—the island has been ruled or invaded by seven different nations!

But let's go 'way back and see who first lived on "the beautiful island." About two thousand years ago some interesting people came in boats from southern Asia. They were not Chinese. These first settlers were small people, brown-skinned. They spoke *dialects* (dialects are different forms of a language) of the *Malayan* language. They belonged to different tribes with strange names like *Atayal* and *Buna*. These settlers were fierce and warlike. Many of them were head-hunters!

Sounds quite a bit like North America when the first white settlers arrived, doesn't it? We might say that these first people were the Indians of Formosa. They are called *aborigines,* which means "the first, or original, people."

The aborigines were and still are much like our Indians. They did not like to farm. They preferred to live in the mountains and jungles. They loved to fish and hunt and fight each other. They did not build large cities. Instead, the aborigines lived in small villages until all the game was killed in that area. Then they moved to a better hunting ground in the mountains.

The aborigines had Formosa to themselves for many years. Then in the year 605 A.D. Chinese explorers discovered the island.

Aborigine girls in tribal dress.

The Chinese are fine sailors. For over two thousand years they have sailed their ships, called *junks,* far and wide. It was natural that they should cross the one hundred miles of ocean to Formosa. But not many Chinese settled there. The warlike aborigines did not welcome strangers. This, too, sounds like our own history, does it not? Some of our early settlers had trouble with our Indians, too.

It was a long time before the Chinese could settle on the island. The early Chinese were either pirates or treasure hunters. In the year 1430, more than fifty years before Christopher Columbus discovered America, Chinese were hunting gold on Formosa.

15

Chinese pagoda and grave. The Chinese discovered Formosa in 605 A.D. but did not settle the island for several centuries.

There were many battles between Chinese and aborigines. And many Chinese sailors and explorers lost their heads! But by the end of the fifteenth century—just about the time Columbus was sailing to the New World—a few Chinese, and Japanese, too, began to live on Formosa. Most of them were pirates. There were Chinese pirates in south Formosa and Japanese pirates in north Formosa.

The pirates fought each other. The aborigines fought each other and the pirates. Formosa was not a very peaceful place.

In fact, the history of Formosa is so filled with fighting and battles that the Chinese have a saying: "Every five years an uprising, every three years a rebellion."

After about 150 years some new adventurers arrived. The Dutch, who were great explorers, sailed their ships into the Straits of Formosa. In 1603 the Dutch occupied the Pescadores Islands. They liked the Pescadores and Formosa too, and decided they would claim all the islands for Holland.

Within twenty-five years the Dutch had built several big forts in southern Formosa. They began to *export* sugar cane to Holland. And then, in 1626, along came a great fleet of Spanish ships. The Spaniards landed in northern Formosa and built big forts there. Now everyone began to fight everyone else. The Chinese did not like the Dutch and fought them. The Dutch and the Spanish fought each other.

As if all this fighting were not enough, a new war began. In the year 1651 a famous Chinese general invaded the Pescadores Islands and Formosa. He came from *Fukien* Province, which is the part of China nearest to Formosa. His name was *Cheng Ch'eng-kung*. But he is better known as *Koxinga*. General Koxinga was one of the greatest generals in Chinese history. And he has become the hero of the Formosan people. With his fleet of war junks, he attacked the Dutch, and after fighting for eleven years, defeated them.

In 1662 General Koxinga established the Kingdom of Formosa. He was the first King. And even though he soon died, thousands of Chinese began to come to the island. They came partly as businessmen and traders. But many came because

China was then being invaded by the fierce *Tartars,* or *Manchus.* Like many of the men and women who first settled America, the thousands of Chinese who came to Formosa were *political refugees.* But for whatever reason they came, they made Formosa a truly Chinese island.

Koxinga was succeeded by his son. But the Kingdom of Formosa did not last long. Within twenty years the Manchus had conquered all of China. They sailed across and conquered Formosa, making it a part of China proper.

But peace did not come to the people of Formosa. It would take a whole book just to write about all the wars. The aborigines rebelled against the Chinese often. There were many pirates. Sometimes the pirates would kidnap sailors from ships that were wrecked along the Formosan coast. Between 1850 and 1860 one hundred and thirty ships were wrecked. Many of the ships belonged to the United States, Great Britain or France. When foreign businessmen or sailors were kidnapped or killed, it made their governments angry!

The warships of other nations came often to try to rescue the crews of wrecked ships. Several times American warships came. And so soldiers and sailors of several nations fought the Chinese.

And then in 1895 China and Japan went to war. The Japanese defeated the Chinese and took Formosa away from them. Japan ruled the island for fifty years. It was not until the end of World War II that Formosa again became a part of China after the United States and its allies had defeated Japan.

The Japanese ruled Formosa harshly. They would not even allow the Chinese to speak their own language. They killed many of the aborigines. But they did establish schools, build highways and railroads. The Japanese built factories and began to mine the rich coal in the mountains. But the people of Formosa always hated the Japanese because of their cruel and harsh rule.

The People

But we are interested in what Formosa is like now. And so our purpose is to learn about the people. What are they like, what do they do and how do they live?

As we have already said, Formosa is a Chinese island and most of the people are Chinese. It might seem from the island's history that there would not be many Chinese. We have been reading about aborigines, Japanese, Spanish and Dutch. But during the past three hundred years many thousands of Chinese have settled on Formosa. They have Chinese customs, they speak Chinese. Formosa is truly, then, a part of China.

But there are several kinds of Chinese, just as there are Americans of Spanish, German or Italian descent. In America we all speak one language. But in Formosa there are several different languages or dialects.

In order to know about the different Chinese on Formosa, let's pretend that we are taking a trip, beginning at the southwestern end of the island and traveling north.

In the far south there are Chinese who came to Formosa from the part of China around Canton. Canton is the largest city in south China. These people speak the *Cantonese* dialect, and there are about 200,000 of them on Formosa.

A Hakka mother and baby.

Farther north we come to villages where the people dress quite differently from the Cantonese. These people are known as the *Hakkas*. Other Chinese call the Hakkas "The Guest People," and they have had an interesting history. Many centuries ago they lived in north China. Then they moved more than two thousand miles to the coast of China opposite the southern end of Formosa. From their new homes on the China coast, many Hakkas sailed across to Formosa. There are now 1,000,000 Hakkas there, and they speak their own language.

Still farther north are the people known as *Hoklos*. There are over 6,000,000 Hoklos. They came from the part of China nearest Formosa and speak a dialect of Chinese called *Amoy*. General Koxinga was part Hoklo. Although there are more Hoklos living in central and north Formosa than elsewhere, they have scattered all over the island. Sometimes you will find a Hoklo village next to a Hakka village; or a Hoklo family living next door to a Cantonese family.

Since 1949, when the Communists conquered China and drove the Nationalist government to Formosa, many other people have come to the island. There are Chinese from far north China, from central China too. Most of these people speak *Mandarin,* which is the official language of China. All children learn to speak Mandarin in school. It is the language used by government officials. It is spoken by all educated people.

But there are still many older people on Formosa who cannot

Hoklo women washing clothes.

speak Mandarin. Most Hoklos cannot speak Hakka, and the Cantonese people in the south cannot talk with either Hakkas or Hoklos. In fact there are sometimes people living next door to each other who cannot understand each other!

The different languages, or dialects, are quite a problem to the Chinese government. However, as people become educated, they will all be speaking the same dialect. And here is a strange thing that helps: No matter what dialect a Chinese speaks, he can *read* Chinese. The written language is the same for all dialects.

In fact, all educated Chinese, Koreans and Japanese can read the same language, even though the spoken languages are entirely different. This is certainly strange, is it not? The written language the same, even though people speak a half dozen different languages!

And so, except for the 150,000 aborigines who still live in the mountains, the people are Chinese. Many cannot speak to each other, customs and dress differ somewhat. But they are all Chinese, just as we Americans are all Americans, regardless of where our ancestors lived.

Formosan Farmers

Like Americans, there are Chinese who live in cities and those who live on farms. There are miners, factory workers, fishermen and farmers. But for the most part, Formosa is a land of farmers. Agriculture is more important than mining or manufacturing. And so if we are really to know what it is like on Formosa, we must study farm life.

Notice the next two pictures, which show a farm village and a typical country scene. In front of the village, in one picture, is a large field, and in the other picture there are several large fields. There is water in these fields. In one picture there are large shocks of grain, while in the other are many small plants. These are rice fields, which you will remember are called paddies.

Rice is by far the most important crop in Formosa. And Formosan rice is considered about the best in Asia. The island has all the things needed for rice farming: rich soil, plenty of water, warm climate. A little later we will learn how the water reaches the fields. But let's first learn something about the life of the most important people on Formosa—the farmers who grow rice.

First, you will be surprised at the size of a Formosan farm. In America our farms cover many acres. A two-hundred-acre farm is not unusual, is it? And in many parts of America we have much larger farms. In Texas and Oklahoma there are ranches that cover thousands of acres.

But in Formosa the average farm covers three or four acres. (The Chinese do not measure land in acres. They use either the term *hectare* or the term *mou*. One hectare is 2.47 acres and one mou is .165 acre.) With farms so tiny you will wonder how it is possible to raise enough food on such small plots!

Look again at the pictures of Formosan farmhouse and village. Notice that the Chinese farmers here have simple homes. Most houses are made of mud, with tiled or sometimes thatched roofs. The farmers do not have tractors, automobiles or trucks. Many farm houses do not have electricity. There are no indoor toilets,

23

A Chinese farmhouse with rice seedlings.

This is a farming village.

no bathtubs, refrigerators or electric stoves. A few farmers have radio sets, but there is no TV on Formosa.

The Chinese are much poorer than we are. Their simple way of life makes it unnecessary to earn a lot of money. Instead of a tractor and a big plow, the Chinese farmer uses a *water buffalo*. The huge, ugly water buffalo pulls the plow. It is the job of the boys and girls to take care of the water buffalo when it is not working. A good water buffalo costs about $75 and is the most valuable possession of a farm family.

The farmer's plow is very simple. All the farm tools are inexpensive. A new tractor, a modern plow, disc and thresher—all the things an American farmer needs cost several thousand dollars. The Chinese farmer has his water buffalo, perhaps a team of oxen too, and a few simple tools that cost altogether perhaps $150 to $200.

The Formosan rice farmer is able to raise two crops of rice each year and one or two other crops. Since nearly all the people in Asia eat rice, he can sell all he does not need for his family. He needs quite a lot for his wife and children, because the Chinese eat rice every meal—even for breakfast! And each member of the family eats several big bowls each meal. In fact each adult member of the family needs between 30 and 40 pounds of rice every month!

On his three or four acres the Chinese farmer can raise plenty of rice. But it is hard work. Every member of the family must help because everything is done by hand. The rice seeds are planted first in little beds. When the seedlings are about six inches high they must be transplanted to the paddies. Later, the rice is

The water buffalo is used for plowing by Formosan families.

harvested by hand. Then it is threshed, sometimes by hand, sometimes by a machine that must be cranked by hand. After that the rice is spread out to dry. Finally it is carried to market on a cart. The cart is pulled either by a water buffalo or by oxen. So you can see that being a rice farmer is hard work!

The Chinese eat other things besides rice. Every farm family has a nice vegetable plot. Nearly all farmers raise pigs, ducks and chickens, and many of them raise turkeys. There are fine fishing grounds along the coast of Formosa, so there is fish in the markets. Thus, besides rice, the Chinese eat fish, meat and several kinds of vegetables.

The favorite vegetable is called *paitsai,* which means "white vegetable." You can often find this vegetable for sale in stores in America. It is called *Chinese cabbage* and looks like celery with very broad stalks and leaves.

In America we do not eat minnows or snails. But the Chinese eat tiny little fish, snails, almost anything that can be found in the water. One of the jobs for small children is to wade around

Every farmhouse has an area for drying rice.

Even small children use chopsticks.

in the water of the paddies, looking for tiny little fish and snails. These are taken home for eating.

In America, beef is probably our favorite meat. We think there is nothing in the world quite as good as a big, juicy beefsteak! But pork is the favorite meat of the Chinese. Poor people will save money just to buy enough pork for one meal. It is always eaten on special festival days. So nearly all Chinese farmers raise pigs. Since there is so much water on Formosa, so many paddy fields and small ponds, there are thousands of ducks and geese. Everybody eats ducks, and duck eggs are eaten just as we eat chicken eggs.

A farm family has lunch, eating with chopsticks.

There is a picture of Chinese eating on this page. Notice the way the family eats. There are no knives or forks on the table. Everyone, even the small children, uses *chopsticks*. Each member of the family has his own bowl of rice. Then in the center of the table are several bowls of vegetables, soup, meat or fish. If someone wants meat or vegetables, he helps himself from the center dishes with chopsticks.

Of course you couldn't very well eat soup with chopsticks, could you? There are spoons for this purpose. But Chinese spoons are not like ours. They are made of *porcelain,* are very short and are shaped a little like boats.

The Chinese people all love a *feast*—a special big meal for special occasions, like our Thanksgiving dinner. There are feasts when someone marries or dies, there are feasts for visiting friends. At a feast there are sometimes very many special dishes. And some of the special dishes might seem very peculiar to Americans. Among feast dishes are *watermelon soup, sharks' fins,* stewed *baby octopus* and *bird's-nest soup.*

Inside of a dock worker's home.

Some Chinese sleep on beds. But the Hakkas use a sleeping platform.

Look at the picture showing the inside of a Chinese house. You can begin to understand how simply the Chinese live. The Hakkas use a *sleeping platform*. Hoklos usually have big beds, but there are no springs, no nice soft mattresses. Many people sleep on boards. And whether the Chinese sleep on beds or platforms, their homes and furnishings are very simple. Houses are much smaller than ours and often are crowded. There is not very much furniture. Except in the cities, and even there not too often, there are no inside bathrooms.

Americans who visit Formosa for the first time often think that all Chinese are dirty. But that is not true. It is just much

31

harder to keep clean. Chinese like to bathe just as we do. During warm weather boys and girls often keep clean by swimming in the rivers and ponds.

But since there are no big bathtubs, no hot-water heaters, it is difficult to take hot baths all the time.

While there is little water in which to bathe, water is very important to the rice farmers. Without water it would not be possible to grow this precious crop. On the opposite page there are two pictures that show how water is brought to the paddies.

The upper picture shows a river in the mountains. On the left-hand side of the river and above it, there is a ditch. The ditch begins high in the mountains and carries the river water for many miles. When the ditch reaches the lowlands, it is joined by similar ditches until there is enough water for a big irrigation ditch like that in the lower picture. There are gates that can be closed to store up water in time of drought, or when the paddies must be dry for harvesting.

Formosa's many mountains help solve the water problem. There are many short, fast-flowing rivers coming off the mountains. The Chinese government has built many dams, with miles of irrigation ditches that bring water to the rice field.

Earlier we read that there are other important crops besides rice. About 60 per cent of all the farm land is devoted to rice. But in the central and southern parts of Formosa there are pineapple and banana plantations. Oranges of several kinds grow everywhere except in the mountains. In central Formosa you will often see great hillsides covered with banana trees or pineapple plants.

Water for rice fields comes from mountain streams.

And in the lowlands there are large irrigation systems.

The rows of bushes are tea plants. Notice the "suspension bridge" across the river.

In fact, if you like fruit, you will be happy on Formosa. Besides those already mentioned, there are several other wonderful fruits. There is one called *papaya,* and there are big, juicy persimmons; plums; many varieties of watermelon.

The Chinese have always been great tea drinkers. They drink tea the way we drink coffee. Many centuries ago Chinese tea became known in Europe. In fact the word "tea" is really a Hoklo word. The first tea to reach Europe, and of course America later on, came from the Hoklo-speaking section of China. In the Hoklo or Amoy language, the word for tea is "dai," pronounced just like "day." From that word we get the word tea.

Tea is important not only because the Chinese like it. It is also exported to other countries. The best tea grows in the high mountains. There are many small tea farms and quite a few large tea plantations. There is a lot of work in growing tea. The bushes must be fertilized and cultivated. Some leaves must be picked off so that those remaining will grow larger. And it is hard work harvesting the tea leaves. Boys and girls do much of this work, helping their parents.

Tea country and also much of the banana and pineapple country is in the mountains. There are not many automobile roads leading into the mountains. In order to bring the crops down, it is necessary to use *narrow-gauge* railroads. These are railroads with tracks a very short distance apart. They are almost like play railroads. Tiny flatcars are used, and often the older boys have the job of pushing the cars up the steep hillsides. Of course coming down is easy!

It is quite a thrill to come zooming down a steep mountainside on one of the little flatcars. There are some places in Formosa where special little railroads lead into the mountains so that tourists can visit the aborigine villages. Through much of the mountain country this is the only way one can travel.

There is one other important crop we should mention, and narrow-gauge railroads are also used to carry this crop to the factories. There are many large sugar-cane plantations in southern Formosa. Fine white sugar is made from the sugar cane. It is an

Narrow-gauge railroad. The little flatcars must be pushed up the mountains.

important crop because nearly all the sugar is sold to other countries.

And there we have the story of Formosa's crops. Rice is most important. Sugar, tea and fruits are also important, especially since these crops can all be sold to other countries. In that way the Chinese government can get the money it needs.

Even though the Chinese on Formosa are poor compared to Americans, they are more fortunate than most people who live in Asia. There is plenty to eat for most people because the rich soil, fine climate and plentiful water make good crops possible. Formosa is one of the few places in Asia where nearly everyone has enough to eat. And it is one of the very few countries where there are no beggars.

Cities and Industries

We have so far been reading about farm life. There are many towns and cities on Formosa. Some of the cities are quite large. *Taipei,* the capital of Formosa, is the largest city. It is situated twelve miles from the sea, near the northern end of the island.

There are five other principal cities and three of these have names quite like that of the capital city. Taipei means "Big North City." In central Formosa there is *Taichung,* which means "Big Central City." On the southern end of the island is *Tainan,* meaning, "Big Southern City." Then on the east coast there is *Taitung.* You will probably guess that this word means "Big Eastern City."

Finally, there are two other important cities, the main seaports on Formosa. *Keelung* is situated on the very northern tip of Formosa, not far from Taipei. On the southwest coast there is another important port city named *Kaohsiung.* If you were traveling to Formosa by ship you would probably land at Keelung. It has a very fine harbor. It was here that the Spanish built their forts, over three hundred years ago.

Taipei, the largest city, has a population of more than 600,000, or approximately that of New Orleans, La., Buffalo, N. Y., or Houston, Texas.

Let's visit Taipei and see what a Formosan city is like. It has been the capital for many years. The Japanese built many fine buildings while they ruled Formosa. Notice the pictures of Taipei. Some of the residential streets are broad and lined with beautiful palm trees.

A street in downtown Taipei.

A palm-lined street in Taipei.

There are some fine homes in Taipei and a few of the downtown stores are quite large. But if you should visit Taipei for long you would begin to notice that it is different from an American city.

For one thing the streets are terribly crowded. There are some cars, jeeps, buses and trucks. There are even ox-carts rolling down the main streets. But the things you would notice are the hundreds of people riding bicycles and a strange-looking thing called a *pedicab*. A pedicab is very much like a rickshaw except that it is pulled by a man riding a bicycle attached to the part where the passenger sits. There is a sort of carriage seat between two big wheels. The bicycle is fastened to the seat part and the pedicab driver "pulls" by pedaling on the bicycle. On the back of the seat there is a covering that can be drawn up in case of rain. It does not cost much to travel by pedicab. To go two miles would cost about twenty-five cents.

There are many pedicabs in the big cities. Most are for hire, just like taxis. But many of the more wealthy people own their own pedicabs just as we own cars. They have their own pedicab "chauffeurs." Some of the private pedicabs are quite fancy, with colored curtains and shiny trimmings.

Of course there are many people who cannot afford to buy a pedicab. Many of these poorer people own bicycles. There are probably as many bicycles in Formosa as in any other country of the same size in the world. Many businessmen pedal to work. Soldiers ride bicycles to their camps, children ride to school and housewives go shopping on their bikes.

Traffic is thick in the cities of Formosa. There are so many

This is a sidewalk market.

different kinds of vehicles, so many people and animals, that one must be very careful when driving a car. And while the main streets are broad, all the side streets are very narrow.

While there are a few big stores, there are many more tiny shops and "open-air markets" right on the sidewalks. Notice the picture of a big vegetable market on the sidewalk. In such places one can buy almost anything needed to eat. Look carefully at the hat the man is wearing. This is the kind of hat most country people wear. It is made of dried banana leaves and has a very broad brim. This helps to keep the rain off. It's a handy sort of a hat to have in a place where there is much rain.

There are also many people who travel about in the cities carrying their "stores" with them. On this page is a picture of a traveling ice-cream man. He carries his ice cream on a platform pulled by a bicycle. Other traveling stores are carried tied to big sticks. Men, women, or even children carry the stores by putting the big sticks across their shoulders.

There are even traveling restaurants! On one end of the carrying stick is a stove that uses charcoal. On the other end is a sort of a cupboard. If anyone wishes to eat, the restaurant-man sets his load down and begins cooking right on the sidewalk!

The traveling ice-cream man!

Inside a shop where tapestries are sold.

The Chinese have always been good at making a living with very simple equipment. Just as there are many traveling merchants, there are many tiny shops. It is not necessary to have much money to operate such a shop because everyone in the family helps. The family lives in the back of the shop so there is no extra rent to pay. There are tiny furniture shops, places where hats are made, shops where fine silks are woven into clothing.

In America most of the things we use in daily life are made in big factories. But in Formosa we find many of these same things made in private homes and shops. For instance, if you want to buy a pair of shoes in Taipei, you probably go to a small shop where a shoemaker takes measurements of your feet. In a few days you go back and there are the shoes! Of course in America you would go to a big shoe store. And the shoes in the store come from a factory where thousands of pairs of shoes are made every day.

Of course there are some big factories in Formosa too. All countries need some factories, or *heavy industry,* as we call it. Formosa is fortunate because the many fast-flowing rivers make it possible to have cheap electricity. Big dams have been built to provide electric power. The dams serve a double purpose: they make electricity, and they provide water for irrigation.

In Formosa there are a number of large factories that make clothing. There are plants that make sugar and can pineapples. There are mills for grinding grain. And there are several important factories to make cheap fertilizer for the farmers.

A land of high mountains might be expected to have some other important resources, might it not? We are thinking of two things: minerals and lumber. Formosa's mineral resources have not been properly explored yet. Coal, gold and sulphur are the most important minerals, and of these coal is by far the most important.

When General Koxinga came to Formosa 300 years ago his men found what they called "black fire-nourishing rocks." This is the name the early Chinese gave to coal. There is much coal, even though it is not of the best variety, and it was coal that caused some of Formosa's early wars. After the steamship was invented, foreign governments became interested in developing Formosan coal mines.

Manufacture of fertilizer is an important industry.

In 1842 a famous American naval officer, Commodore Perry, arrived in Keelung harbor to investigate the "black fire-nourishing rocks." He found that it could be bought for one dollar a ton. A few years later the British also became interested in Formosan coal. But the Chinese government refused to allow the British or anyone else to mine the precious black rock.

The Chinese rulers of Formosa claimed that the dragons which, according to legend, had made Formosa thousands of years ago, still lived in the mountains. If any mining was done, the dragons' tails or feet might be hurt. And of course that would make the dragons mad. They might cause earthquakes and many other disasters! And so the Imperial Court of China decided that the "mining of coal was absolutely and for all eternity prohibited."

But foreign countries needed coal for their ships that went to the Far East. A few years after the Chinese had forbidden the British to mine, a French warship arrived in Keelung harbor. When the Chinese refused to allow any coal mining, the French began to shoot with their big guns. They got coal!

Ever since that time, coal has been mined. It is used for Formosa's factories and is also shipped to other countries. Each year shiploads of Formosan coal go to Japan and Korea. It has become, like sugar, an important export.

While the dragons kept coal from being mined, the high, steep mountains have made lumbering difficult. The picture on the next page shows a huge log being lowered down the side of a mountain. There are millions of big trees like this in the high mountains. The Chinese government is trying to build roads into the mountains so that the trees can be brought out.

There is fine hardwood for building houses and furniture. There is a tree called *camphor* which is very important, too. Camphor trees produce fine wood and an oil called camphor oil. Formosa produces more of this oil than any other country in the world. And there are also many soft-wood trees from which paper can be manufactured.

We have now seen how Formosa's resources are being developed. Compared to the United States it is not a rich land. But considering its small size, Formosa is a very rich island. It produces food, enough to feed its own people and enough left over to sell to other countries. It has coal, lumber, rivers that can pro-

45

There is much lumber in the mountains.

duce electricity. Formosa is rich and prosperous compared to many other small countries. It is for this reason that Formosa is so important now.

The Government of Formosa

This might be a good place to see what kind of government our Formosan ally has. You have studied about different kinds of governments in the world. There are republics like the United States; there are monarchies, or nations ruled by kings; there are dictatorships.

Japan, for instance, is a monarchy. It has an Emperor, but the real power lies in the elected representatives. So we call Japan a constitutional monarchy. The Republic of the Philippines is a democracy very much like ours. The Nationalist government on Formosa is also a republic. Its official name is the Republic of China.

There is a National Assembly elected by the people every six years. The Assembly then elects the president. The people elect their mayors and councilmen. But unlike America, where there are always two strong political parties, there is only one strong party in Free China. It is called the *Kuomintang*. This means "the People's Party."

In spite of threat of war, the government of China has helped its people on Formosa. They have freedom from want. They have the right to elect their own local officials. Over 80 per cent of the people vote in each election on Formosa.

Formosa's capitol building.

Religions and Superstitions

There are many Christians on Formosa. Some are Protestants, many are Catholics. But it would be incorrect to say that Formosa is a Christian land.

Like their fellow countrymen in mainland China, the Formosans include *Buddhists, Taoists* and some *Mohammedans*. Probably most people believe in some of the teachings of Buddhism, some in the ideas of *Taoism* and also those of *Confucius,* a wise Chinese who lived many centuries ago.

There are many temples on Formosa. Every town has at least one. Many people go to the temples to worship. There are huge images of Buddha and many other gods in the temples. There is one very popular goddess called the Goddess of Mercy. Another goddess is one who is supposed to protect all sailors. Her name is Ma Chu and the story of how she became a goddess is interesting. According to Chinese legend Ma Chu lived many hundreds of years ago. Her father and her brothers sailed junks along the China coast. One day Ma Chu fell asleep while she was weaving. She had a dream that her father and brothers were in a terrible storm and were about to be swept against rocks.

Ma Chu caught the rope of the junk in which her father sailed and held it in her teeth. With her hands she caught her brothers' two ships. She was dragging all three junks to safety when she heard her mother calling. Being an obedient girl, she opened her mouth to answer her mother. When Ma Chu awakened from her dream she was very sad. She felt that her father and brothers must be in great trouble.

In a few days the news came that her father's junk had been lost in a great storm. Her brothers' two junks had been saved in some strange way! Ma Chu then told the neighbors about her dream. She believed that her father's junk had been lost because she opened her mouth to answer her mother's call.

From that day on, Ma Chu has been the goddess of all Chinese who sail ships. There are many special temples in her honor. When ships are in a storm, the sailors all pray to Ma Chu. If the storm is very bad, they throw offerings into the sea. Some Chinese junks even have little images of Ma Chu in their bows.

There are many other gods and goddesses worshiped by the Chinese. People go to the temples to make offerings of food and money. They burn *incense* before the images.

The Chinese who are not Christians, and even some of the Christians, are very superstitious. They believe there are many evil spirits and devils in the world. Many people still believe that sickness is caused by devils or evil spirits. They not only go to the temples to make offerings so that the evil spirits will not bother them. They have ways of fooling the evil spirits. Since boys are considered much more important than girls, the Chinese believe that the devils of sickness are more interested in the boys. Sometimes they will give a girl's name to a boy! In this way they think that the evil spirits and devils will be fooled and will not bother the boy.

As more and more people become educated, fewer believe in evil spirits. Also there are more and more Christians among the Chinese and even among the aborigines. Often now, if you visit a temple, you will find it falling to pieces. People are slowly

A household altar. Notice the pictures of gods.

learning that sickness, for instance, is caused by germs and not by devils. The picture on this page shows the inside of a home with some of the gods and spirits worshiped by the family.

The aborigines are even more superstitious than the Chinese. They too have their special devils, gods and evil spirits.

Many of the aborigines do not speak Chinese. While the Japanese ruled Formosa, they made the aborigines learn their language. And since it has not been many years since the Japanese were defeated, many of the aborigines still speak Japanese.

The aborigines of course have their own languages and dialects. But since the boys and girls in school study Chinese, it will not be too many years before they can all speak Chinese.

Most of the aborigines still live in the wild mountains. But they are no longer head-hunters! They live in small villages tucked away in the jungle. As their ancestors did, they will live in one area until all the game is gone. Then they move on to another place.

The aborigines are very brave fighters. They caused the harsh Japanese a great deal of trouble. One time, not too many years ago, the aborigines killed and chopped off the heads of 200 Japanese soldiers. The Chinese government does not want to have that kind of trouble! It has tried hard to make friends with the mountain people. No Chinese are allowed to settle in the high mountains. These mountains are reserved for the aborigines.

There are many Christian churches in Formosa.

Modern aborigine women, and below, aborigine girls in an ancient tribal dance.

However, the Chinese government encourages the mountain people to settle in the plains. They are being taught to be better farmers. Along the mountainous east coast of Formosa, the Chinese government provides them with big motor boats and nets and teaches them how to catch fish in the ocean.

Because of this friendly attitude, there is peace now between the aborigines and the Chinese. Some aborigines are marrying Chinese. They have learned to vote in elections. Quite a number are moving out of the mountains, to become farmers and fishermen. The Chinese call those who still live in the mountains "raw savages." Those who are becoming civilized are called "ripe savages."

Going to School

The children of Formosa, whether they are aborigines or Chinese, are in many ways like the children of America. Their lives are more difficult, perhaps. There are very few families with money for expensive toys. There are thousands of Formosan children who have never seen a movie. No one has ever seen TV. Many children have never had a ride in an automobile. But they go to school, they have games, they play just like American children.

The day begins early for a Chinese family. That is especially true of those who live on a farm. Father must get up at daylight. If it is rice-planting time or harvesting time, everyone must help. And there are special jobs for the children.

The family water buffalo must get his daily mud bath. And

53

it is the job of one of the children to ride the big animal to the nearest pond or mudhole. The buffaloes are never happy unless they can wallow in the mud or water for an hour or so each day. They like to get covered with water until only the tip of the nose and the eyes are showing.

There are many other jobs for children on the farm. Where ducks and geese are raised, the children help take care of them. It is quite a job to herd a flock of three or four hundred ducks! Since nearly all children go to school, these special jobs must be done early in the morning or after school.

School begins early and lasts until four or five o'clock. There are no school buses so nearly everyone walks to school. Some of the big boys have bikes. And in the cities a few rich people send their children to school in the family pedicab. Children study many of the same subjects American children study.

But there are some differences. All children must of course study Mandarin, the national language of China. And they must learn how to write in Chinese. This is much more difficult than learning our alphabet. Let's see what a Chinese word, or *character,* looks like. One of the most common family names, or surnames, in Formosa is *Lin.* Sometimes it is spelled *Ling.*

This word means "forest"; so a Mr. Lin is Mr. Forest. What makes a forest? Several trees, or many trees, of course. The Chinese word for tree is written like this: 木 . To make the word for Lin, the Chinese put two trees together like this: 林 . So you see that the Chinese written language is a sort of a picture language. And it is very difficult to learn to read and write it correctly. Some words, however, are rather easy to write. On this page are some Chinese numbers. It might be fun to see if you can learn to write some of the numbers.

SOME CHINESE NUMBERS

一	One
二	Two
三	Three
四	Four
五	Five
六	Six
七	Seven
八	Eight
九	Nine
十	Ten
十一	Eleven
十二	Twelve
二十	Twenty
二十一	Twenty-one

There are several differences between an American and a Chinese school. For one thing, Chinese children often study out loud! Sometimes all the children in a class will be doing this, in a sing-song fashion. A Chinese school is often a noisy place. Another difference is that nearly all school children wear a special school *uniform*.

Just as in America, Chinese children have clubs. In the cities and towns there are boy and girl scouts. In the country many children belong to the 4-H club. In some places there are special 4-H clubhouses. And the 4-H members have contests and projects of many kinds.

After school is out there is nearly always work to be done at home. But there is always time for play, too. Chinese children have some games like ours. The boys love to fly kites, or go swimming. There is one very simple game played by kicking a big rubber ball.

The Chinese love picnics, too. They especially like to go places where there are boats. Near Taipei there is a place called Green Lake. It is really only a broad place in the Tamsui river. There are many covered boats and on a nice week end families go to Green Lake to enjoy boating and picnicking.

The most famous vacation or picnic place in Formosa is Sun-Moon Lake. Only people who can afford to take long trips can visit this beautiful place in the mountains. There are good hotels and boats can be rented. On the far side of the lake there is an aborigine village. Visitors to Sun-Moon Lake often go across the lake to see the aborigines.

Chinese love picnics and boating.

Sun-Moon Lake is a popular vacation place in the mountains.

Travel and Transportation

When a family travels from Taipei to Sun-Moon Lake, a distance of 150 miles, how do they travel? While it is common for country people to walk many miles to visit friends or the nearest village, there are fine highways and railways too.

Notice the picture of a highway and an ox-cart. Many people in the country travel and transport their goods on ox-carts. But there are buses, and on the railways there are fast trains.

You will remember that the east coast of Formosa is very rugged. The mountains there fall right into the sea. There are few railroads along that coast. But along the flat west coast there are both railroads and highways.

We have mentioned already that there are not many highways going into the mountains, but these few roads are interesting. There are many fast-flowing rivers to cross. Nearly all the rivers are crossed by suspension bridges. These bridges hang on giant cables.

There is a picture of a suspension bridge on page 34. There are suspension bridges for cars and suspension bridges for people to walk across. Since too many cars might break the cable, a policeman must stand guard at each end of a bridge so that only one car at a time may cross. Even then the bridge sways from side to side!

Besides highways and railways, Formosa has an excellent airlines system. There are many airfields, and since the island is only 240 miles long it is possible to visit any part of the island in a few hours. A traveler can leave Taipei in the morning and

There are good highways in Formosa but ox-carts are often used for transportation of goods.

make a round-the-island trip, returning the same afternoon. The plane flies across the high mountains to the east coast. It stops at cities along the coast, then crosses to the west coast. Passenger planes even fly out to the Pescadores Islands lying off the west coast.

Air travel on Formosa is important because many of the cities on the east coast would be hard to reach otherwise. The main airline is operated by a famous American airman, General Claire Chennault. All the pilots are Americans.

You will be surprised at how quickly one can reach Formosa from the United States. There are planes leaving San Francisco,

Los Angeles and Seattle almost every day. And it takes only forty hours to travel all the way to Formosa.

Flying across the Pacific, the plane crosses the international date line. This is a place in the middle of the ocean where each day first begins. Going one way, the traveler loses a day. Going the other way, one day is gained. Because of this, I once celebrated New Year's Day on Formosa, then left by plane for America and forty hours later I had another New Year's celebration in America!

Holidays and Festivals

We Americans have our special holidays and festivals. Chinese have their special days too. There are religious festivals, and special days to celebrate important dates in Chinese history.

The most important holiday for the Chinese is New Year's Day. However, they have two New Year's Days! They celebrate January First, just as we do. But Chinese have an even bigger celebration on the *Chinese New Year*. This day is also called the *Lunar New Year*. Many Chinese use the old calendar based exactly on the moon. The first day of each new moon is the first day of the new month.

Chinese New Year's Day generally falls in late January. Everyone dresses up. There are parties. Boys and girls exchange gifts. People who can afford to do so give big feasts.

Old-style Chinese celebrate special days for almost every month of the lunar year. One of the most interesting special days is the Dragon Boat Festival. It comes on the fifth day of the fifth month, or according to our calendar, during early June. The Dragon Boat Festival lasts for five days. Everyone has a wonderful time, especially at the Dragon Boat races. The boats are made very long and narrow. At the front end is a big carved dragon. The boat is supposed to be in the shape of a dragon. About twenty young men are in each boat. In the center of each boat there are men with drums and gongs. So there is a lot of noise while the boats race. And nearly always one of the boatmen falls into the water.

Like many Chinese festivals, the Dragon Boat Festival has

Chinese festivals are colorful.

been going on for many centuries. According to Chinese legend there was once a very wise minister in the court of an Emperor. The minister saw that there were many things wrong in China. He urged that changes be made so that the people would have better government. The faithful minister was dismissed and was so sad that he committed suicide by jumping into a river. Ever since that time, 2,400 years ago, the Dragon Boats are supposed to go out and search for the soul of the brave minister!

The most important national holiday is on the tenth of October. It is a day of celebration just like our July Fourth. Since October is the tenth month of the year, the October Tenth celebration is called "Double Ten." Double Ten celebrates the first successful battles in the revolution against the Manchus, who ruled China until 1911. There are patriotic speeches and parades. The National flag flies everywhere.

When the Chinese celebrate anything, they do it with fire-crackers. Holidays, festivals, weddings and even funerals are celebrated with firecrackers. An especially important festival sounds like a battle!

Formosan Heroes

The Chinese have their national heroes, too, just as we do. For all Chinese, whether they live on Formosa or in China, there is one special hero. He is Dr. Sun Yat-sen, who led the revolution against the Emperors of China many years ago.

Dr. Sun died in 1925. But his picture is still found in schools and all public buildings. He is considered the George Washington of China. But for the people of Formosa there are also special heroes connected with Formosan history.

The greatest of these is General Koxinga, the Chinese general who defeated the Dutch in the seventeenth century. There are many legends about Koxinga. He not only fought and defeated the Dutch. For twenty-five years he also fought the Manchus, or Tartars, who were invading China.

When Koxinga came ashore on Formosa 300 years ago it is said that he waded through the water and walked across a wide, sandy beach. According to Chinese legend all his footprints in the sand turned to fish. And that is why, say the Chinese, there is such good fishing in the ocean around Formosa.

One time Koxinga's army was besieged on the top of a mountain. There was no water on the top of the mountain. The soldiers were dying of thirst. Koxinga then drove his sword into the earth and prayed for water. According to legend, a great spring of water gushed out of the earth. To this day the mountain is called Iron Sword Mountain.

Chinese children study about Koxinga because he was a great patriot and a great soldier. But they study about the life of another hero for a different reason.

You will remember that the aborigines once were headhunters. The Chinese rulers of Formosa tried for many years to stop head-hunting. But all their efforts were unsuccessful until a man named Wu Feng solved the problem. Wu Feng was a magistrate in the mountains. This means that he was the representative of the Chinese government. He was an honest ruler and the aborigines liked him.

But even Magistrate Wu Feng could not persuade the mountain people to stop fighting and taking heads—until he tried something special. One day he called all the aborigine chiefs together and told them that he had orders from the Imperial government that head-hunting must stop. He explained that he would allow the chiefs to cut off one more head. After that, any aborigine caught head-hunting would lose his own head!

Wu Feng told the chiefs that on a certain evening they should gather at a place in the mountains where two trails crossed. Just after dark a man dressed in white would walk down one of the trails. The aborigines would be allowed to kill the stranger in white and cut off his head. After that there would be no more head-hunting.

The mountain people thought this was a strange business, but they agreed because they loved Magistrate Wu. On the evening selected, they gathered at the crossroads. Soon after dark, a figure dressed in white walked down the trail. The aborigine chiefs gave a great war cry and killed the man. His head was cut off. Then torches were lit so that there could be a procession to the village.

When the light from the torches shone upon the head that had been cut off there was a great gasp. The aborigines had killed their beloved magistrate, Wu Feng! Everyone was very unhappy. The chiefs agreed that they would not take any more heads. They realized that Wu Feng had given his life so that they would learn that head-hunting was wrong. Except for the days of harsh Japanese rule, the aborigines have kept their promise.

The story of Wu Feng is a true story. He knew that the mountain people must have a shock if they were ever to stop head-hunting. And so he gave his life that they might learn. If you travel in the Formosan mountains you will see many little shrines and temples built in memory of Wu Feng, the magistrate who gave his life that others might live.

Chinese school children read about Wu Feng so that they too can learn the need for self-sacrifice. Chinese soldiers study the life of General Koxinga and the story of Wu Feng. It is thought that if everyone, especially soldiers, can learn the lessons taught by these two men, China will always remain free.

America is helping to train Chinese soldiers like this.

A new power plant built with American help.

Formosa's Future

There are many soldiers on Formosa. If you travel about the island, you will see bomb shelters and trenches everywhere. Even in Taipei, the capital city, there are fortifications on many street corners. Along the beaches there are guns and tanks and barbed wire.

Even the children must learn something about military life. The boys drill and learn how to march. There are many Civilian Defense workers. There are air raid alarms when everyone must go to the nearest shelter.

For as we have mentioned before, the Chinese government on

Formosa must always be prepared for attack. The United States has promised to help the people of Formosa defend their island. It is our hope, however, that the trouble can be settled without war.

There are several thousand Americans on Formosa, helping the Chinese in many ways. American farm experts are teaching Chinese farmers. Other Americans are helping to build factories. This is a part of the American economic aid program. Our government helps many other countries in the same way, so that the people may have better lives.

A Chinese farmer opens a bag of fertilizer, a gift from America.

So you see that Americans and Chinese are working together to make Formosa a better place to live, to make it strong, and to keep its people healthy and happy.

Chinese children selling fruit on the street smile goodbye.

History

A.D. 605   Chinese record unsuccessful expeditions to Formosa.

1430   Chinese begin recording history of the island and begin explorations.

1592   Pirates, Chinese and Japanese, active.

1603   Dutch naval ships take shelter in Pescadores.

1615   Japanese attempt conquest.

1620-1624   Dutch settlements.

1626   Spanish establish Fort Santissimus Trinidad at Keelung.

1626-1627   Fighting between Japanese settlers and Dutch.

1640-1642   Fighting between Dutch and Spanish.

1651   General Koxinga attacks Dutch who finally surrender in 1662.

1662   Koxinga establishes Kingdom.

1663   Dutch recapture Keelung but abandon Formosa in 1668.

1683   Formosa conquered by the Manchus and becomes part of Fukien Province.

1696   First rebellion against the Manchus.

1720-1820   Period of continuous rebellions and civil war.

1830   War between Hakkas and Hoklos.

1854   U.S.S. *Macedonian* from Perry's Squadron searches for American sailors believed to be slaves on Formosa.

1855   First trader, an American, begins operation.

1860-1870   Period of considerable trade with western nations.

1867   Two American warships land men looking for Americans captured by Formosan pirates.

1874   Japanese invade Formosa but withdraw.

1877   Spain threatens invasion.

1884-1885   War with France during which parts of Formosa are invaded and blockaded.

1894-1895   War between China and Japan results in ceding of Formosa to Japan.

1895   Formosans form republics, one in north and one in south.

1895-1902   Continuous uprisings against the Japanese.

1941   Beginning of World War II. Formosa becomes major base for Japanese attacks on the Philippines.

1945   Formosa again becomes Chinese territory.

1949   Nationalist government retreats to Formosa.

1954   Continuous bombardment of Quemoy Island by the Communists.

1955   Mutual Defense Treaty between U.S. and Nationalist China in which U.S. pledges to help defend Formosa.

Facts

Population: approximately 10,000,000.

Area: 13,886 square miles, which includes Formosa and approximately 80 smaller islands.

Two-thirds of Formosa is mountainous with seventy-seven peaks exceeding 10,000 feet in altitude. Twenty-three per cent of the land is cultivated.

Climate: tropical in the south, sub-tropical over greater part of the island.

Crops: Two-thirds of the arable land is in rice. Other important crops are sugar, fruits, tea. Fifty-five per cent of the population is engaged in farming.

Source and Reference Books

Report from Formosa by H. Maclear Bate (E. P. Dutton, 1952).
Formosa Beachhead by Geraldine Fitch (Regnery, 1953).
Formosa by Joseph W. Ballantine (Brookings Institution, 1952).
Still the Rice Grows Green by John C. Caldwell (Regnery, 1955).
Rural Taiwan—Problem and Promise by Arthur F. Raper.

(This and other excellent publications on Formosa are published by The Joint Commission on Rural Reconstruction, International Cooperation Administration, APO 63, c/o Postmaster, San Francisco.)